...when someone ask me who the hell
I think I am when I`m shopping...

"Whoever said that money can`t buy happiness,
simply didn`t know where to go shopping"
Bo Derek

This book belongs to:

"Online shopping is a great way t
compare prices, find bargains and
save money from anywhere with
an internet or mobile data
connection. But as its popularity
has increased, so have the risks,
with more and more people trying
to scam you out of your money or
steal your card details. Thankfully
if you follow a few simple rules
you can have a safe and secure
online shopping experience."

MR PINKY FOX

www.moneyhelper.org.u

MR Pinky Fox:
My account orders placed
Online Shopping Tracker

Copyright ©2021 by
Mr Pinky Fox
ISBN: 9798547166938

This book, art or any portion thereof may not be reproduced
used in any manner whatsoever without the written permission
the publisher except for the use of brief quotations in reviews a
certain other non-commercial uses, as permitted by copyright la

Table of contents:

Online shopping safety tips

These are some really simple ways to shop safely online you can use every day:

- Research retailers online to make sure they're legitimate.
- Make sure the website is secure.
- Know your rights and the company's returns policy.
- Keep software and virus protection up-to-date and use strong passwords for online accounts.
- Don't use public wi-fi. Your standard data connection is more secure.
- Pay using a credit card. You'll have more protection. Or use online services such as PayPal – so scammers can't get hold of your bank details.
- Be smart. If a deal looks too good to be true, it probably is.

Source: https://www.moneyhelper.org.uk/en/everyday-money/banking/shop-safely-online

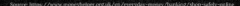

The 5 best places to buy groceries online in 2021

Shopping for groceries online can be a convenient way to save time.
Instacart is widely available nationwide without a membership fee, and you can "shop" locally.
Many services have policies to reduce social interactions and support the shopper community.
Online grocery shopping is an incredibly convenient way to shop while avoiding crowded aisles and rogue shopping carts in the parking lot. Though it's not for those who want to pick their own fruit or get the double coupon discount on pasta, shopping for your groceries online is a great way to save time if you're willing to relinquish some control.

Of course, you should expect to pay a bit more than you would if you shopped yourself. Most online grocery stores and delivery programs include subscription costs, delivery fees, and the option to tip your shopper or driver — which we suggest you do. Some services have steeper fees than others, but all are convenient ways to get what you need.

Here are the **best places to buy groceries online** in 2021:

- Best online grocery store for shopping local: **Instacart**
- Best online grocery store for bulk items: **Boxed**
- Best online grocery store on a budget: **Walmart**
- Best online grocery store for Amazon Prime members: **Amazon Fresh**
- Best online grocery store for organic groceries: **Thrive Market**

Source: https://www.businessinsider.com/best-online-grocery-store?IR=T

Shopping List

BUDGET

TOP TIP:
IF YOU'RE BUYING AN EXPENSIVE ITEM, CHECK THE MANUFACTURERS WEBSITE TO
MAKE SURE YOU'RE USING AN AUTHORISED DISTRIBUTOR OR SELLER.

My Order Placed Tracker

Order Date	Product Description	Shopping Platform	Tracking	Ship Date	Total Cost	Maximum Return Date

PROTECT YOURSELF WHILE SHOPPING FOR ESSENTIALS

Go early morning or late
night when fewer people
are likely to be there.

SOURCE: CDC.GOV

My Order Placed Tracker

Order Date	Product Description	Shopping Platform	Tracking	Ship Date	Total Cost	Maximum Return Date

Weekly Meal Plan

Monday

Breakfast /
Lunch /
Dinner /

Saturday

Breakfast /
Lunch /
Dinner /

Tuesday

Breakfast /
Lunch /
Dinner /

Sunday

Breakfast /
Lunch /
Dinner /

Wednesday

Breakfast /
Lunch /
Dinner /

Shopping List

Thursday

Breakfast /
Lunch /
Dinner /

Friday

Breakfast /
Lunch /
Dinner /

My Order Placed Tracker

Order Date	Product Description	Shopping Platform	Tracking	Ship Date	Total Cost	Maximum Return Date

Monthly Meal Plan

Mon	Tues	Wed	Thurs	Fri	Sat/Sun

New to try

Shopping List

My Order Placed Tracker

Order Date	Product Description	Shopping Platform	Tracking	Ship Date	Total Cost	Maximum Return Date

Recommended
Groceries

- [ ] Grass-fed beef
- [ ] Salmon
- [ ] Chicken breasts
- [ ] Avocado oil
- [ ] Extra virgin olive oil
- [ ] Coconut oil
- [ ] Butter
- [ ] Heavy cream
- [ ] Avocados
- [ ] Spinach

- [ ] Lemons
- [ ] Blueberries
- [ ] Raspberries
- [ ] Celery
- [ ] Mushrooms
- [ ] Walnuts
- [ ] Almonds
- [ ] Flaxseed
- [ ] Chia seeds
- [ ] Almond flour

- [ ] Feta cheese
- [ ] Goats milk
- [ ] Bone broth
- [ ] Green tea
- [ ] Stevia
- [ ] Vanilla essence
- [ ] Cinnamon
- [ ] Hymalayan salt
- [ ] Paprika
- [ ] Chilli flakes

<u>NOTES</u>

My Order Placed Tracker

Order Date	Product Description	Shopping Platform	Tracking	Ship Date	Total Cost	Maximum Return Date

 # GROCERY # ORDER TRACKER

MONTH OF			YEAR	
DATE	ORDER #	QUANTITY	PRODUCT	$

My Order Placed Tracker

Order Date	Product Description	Shopping Platform	Tracking	Ship Date	Total Cost	Maximum Return Date

SHOPPING HABITS TRACKER

MONTH OF

HABIT:

1	2	3	4	5	6	7	8	9	10	11
12	13	14	15	16	17	18	19	20	21	22
23	24	25	26	27	28	29	30	31		

GOAL: **DONE:** **REWARD:**

HABIT:

1	2	3	4	5	6	7	8	9	10	11
12	13	14	15	16	17	18	19	20	21	22
23	24	25	26	27	28	29	30	31		

GOAL: **DONE:** **REWARD:**

HABIT:

1	2	3	4	5	6	7	8	9	10	11
12	13	14	15	16	17	18	19	20	21	22
23	24	25	26	27	28	29	30	31		

GOAL: **DONE:** **REWARD:**

HABIT:

1	2	3	4	5	6	7	8	9	10	11
12	13	14	15	16	17	18	19	20	21	22
23	24	25	26	27	28	29	30	31		

GOAL: **DONE:** **REWARD:**

HABIT:

1	2	3	4	5	6	7	8	9	10	11
12	13	14	15	16	17	18	19	20	21	22
23	24	25	26	27	28	29	30	31		

GOAL: **DONE:** **REWARD:**

My Order Placed Tracker

Order Date	Product Description	Shopping Platform	Tracking	Ship Date	Total Cost	Maximum Return Date

SHOPPING HABITS TRACKER

MONTH OF

HABIT:

1	2	3	4	5	6	7	8	9	10	11
12	13	14	15	16	17	18	19	20	21	22
23	24	25	26	27	28	29	30	31		

GOAL: **DONE:** **REWARD:**

HABIT:

1	2	3	4	5	6	7	8	9	10	11
12	13	14	15	16	17	18	19	20	21	22
23	24	25	26	27	28	29	30	31		

GOAL: **DONE:** **REWARD:**

HABIT:

1	2	3	4	5	6	7	8	9	10	11
12	13	14	15	16	17	18	19	20	21	22
23	24	25	26	27	28	29	30	31		

GOAL: **DONE:** **REWARD:**

HABIT:

1	2	3	4	5	6	7	8	9	10	11
12	13	14	15	16	17	18	19	20	21	22
23	24	25	26	27	28	29	30	31		

GOAL: **DONE:** **REWARD:**

HABIT:

1	2	3	4	5	6	7	8	9	10	11
12	13	14	15	16	17	18	19	20	21	22
23	24	25	26	27	28	29	30	31		

GOAL: **DONE:** **REWARD:**

My Order Placed Tracker

Order Date	Product Description	Shopping Platform	Tracking	Ship Date	Total Cost	Maximum Return Date

My Notes

Sun Mon Tue Wed Thu Fri Sat

BUDGET

My Order Placed Tracker

Order Date	Product Description	Shopping Platform	Tracking	Ship Date	Total Cost	Maximum Return Date

BUDGET

My Order Placed Tracker

Order Date	Product Description	Shopping Platform	Tracking	Ship Date	Total Cost	Maximum Return Date

My Notes

☀ ☁ ☂ ❄   Sun Mon Tue Wed Thu Fri Sat

BUDGET

My Order Placed Tracker

Order Date	Product Description	Shopping Platform	Tracking	Ship Date	Total Cost	Maximum Return Date

Shopping List

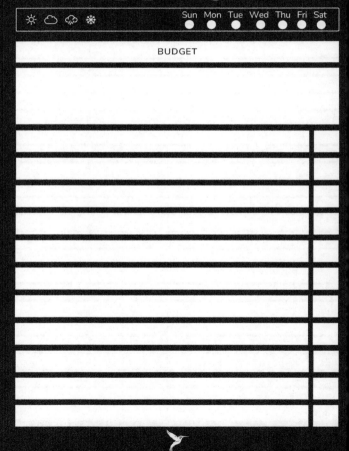

☀ ☁ ☂ ❄　　　　Sun Mon Tue Wed Thu Fri Sat

BUDGET

My Order Placed Tracker

Order Date	Product Description	Shopping Platform	Tracking	Ship Date	Total Cost	Maximum Return Date

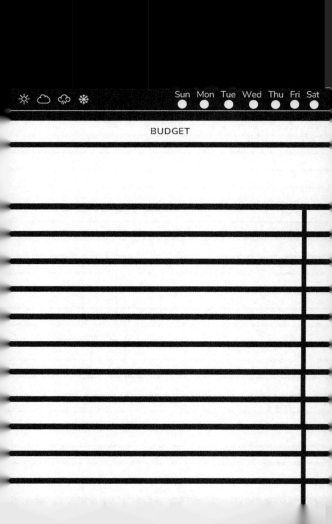

BUDGET

My Order Placed Tracker

Order Date	Product Description	Shopping Platform	Tracking	Ship Date	Total Cost	Maximum Return Date

Shopping List

☀ ☁ ☔ ❄

	Sun	Mon	Tue	Wed	Thu	Fri	Sat
	●	●	●	●	●	●	●

BUDGET

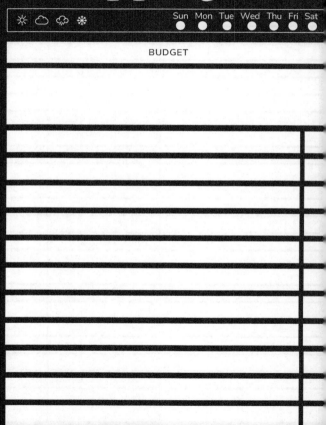

My Order Placed Tracker

Order Date	Product Description	Shopping Platform	Tracking	Ship Date	Total Cost	Maximum Return Date

My Notes

Sun Mon Tue Wed Thu Fri Sat

BUDGET

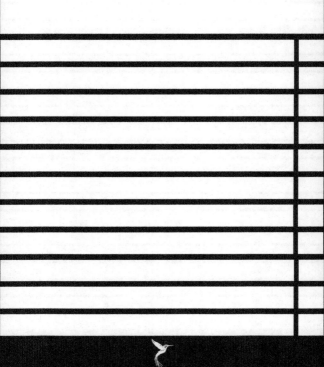

My Order Placed Tracker

Order Date	Product Description	Shopping Platform	Tracking	Ship Date	Total Cost	Maximum Return Date

Shopping List

Sun Mon Tue Wed Thu Fri Sat

BUDGET

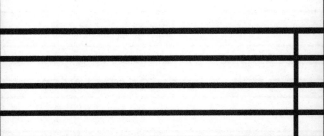

My Order Placed Tracker

Order Date	Product Description	Shopping Platform	Tracking	Ship Date	Total Cost	Maximum Return Date

My Notes

BUDGET	

My Order Placed Tracker

Order Date	Product Description	Shopping Platform	Tracking	Ship Date	Total Cost	Maximum Return Date

Shopping List

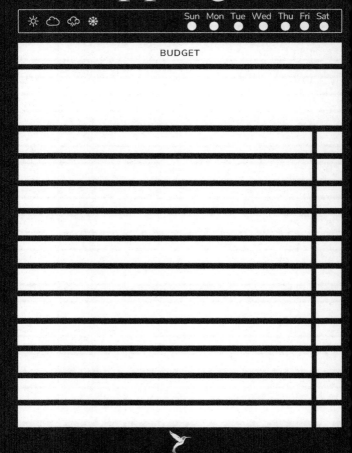

☀ ☁ ☔ ❄	Sun Mon Tue Wed Thu Fri Sat

BUDGET

My Order Placed Tracker

Order Date	Product Description	Shopping Platform	Tracking	Ship Date	Total Cost	Maximum Return Date

My Notes

Sun Mon Tue Wed Thu Fri Sat

BUDGET

My Order Placed Tracker

Order Date	Product Description	Shopping Platform	Tracking	Ship Date	Total Cost	Maximum Return Date

Shopping List

Sun	Mon	Tue	Wed	Thu	Fri	Sat
●	●	●	●	●	●	●

BUDGET	

My Order Placed Tracker

Order Date	Product Description	Shopping Platform	Tracking	Ship Date	Total Cost	Maximum Return Date

My Notes

☀ ☁ ⛆ ❄   Sun Mon Tue Wed Thu Fri Sat
                ● ● ● ● ● ● ●

BUDGET

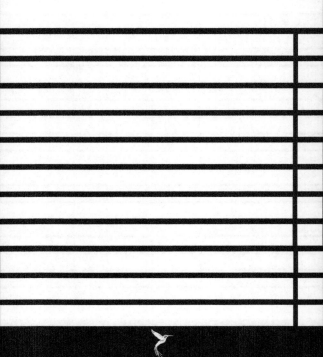

My Order Placed Tracker

Order Date	Product Description	Shopping Platform	Tracking	Ship Date	Total Cost	Maximum Return Date

Shopping List

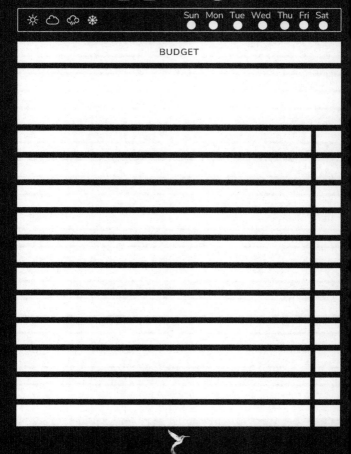

Sun Mon Tue Wed Thu Fri Sat

BUDGET

My Order Placed Tracker

Order Date	Product Description	Shopping Platform	Tracking	Ship Date	Total Cost	Maximum Return Date

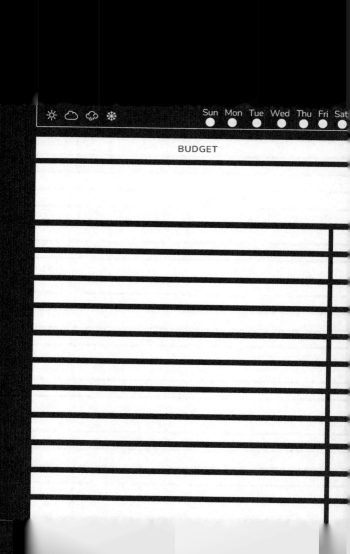

BUDGET

Sun Mon Tue Wed Thu Fri Sat

My Order Placed Tracker

Order Date	Product Description	Shopping Platform	Tracking	Ship Date	Total Cost	Maximum Return Date

Shopping List

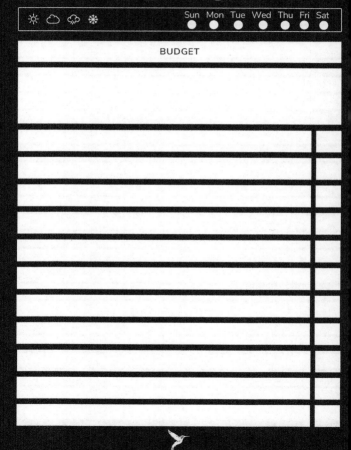

	Sun	Mon	Tue	Wed	Thu	Fri	Sat
☀ ☁ 🌧 ❄	●	●	●	●	●	●	●

BUDGET

My Order Placed Tracker

Order Date	Product Description	Shopping Platform	Tracking	Ship Date	Total Cost	Maximum Return Date

My Notes

Sun Mon Tue Wed Thu Fri Sat

BUDGET

My Order Placed Tracker

Order Date	Product Description	Shopping Platform	Tracking	Ship Date	Total Cost	Maximum Return Date

Shopping List

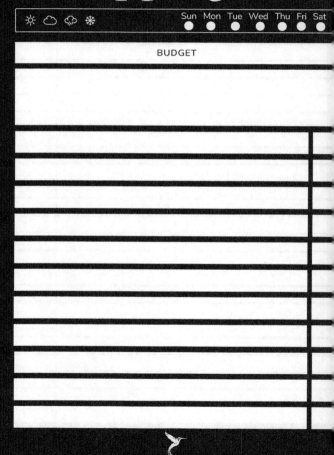

| ☀ ☁ ☂ ❄ | Sun | Mon | Tue | Wed | Thu | Fri | Sat |

BUDGET

My Order Placed Tracker

Order Date	Product Description	Shopping Platform	Tracking	Ship Date	Total Cost	Maximum Return Date

My Notes

BUDGET

My Order Placed Tracker

Order Date	Product Description	Shopping Platform	Tracking	Ship Date	Total Cost	Maximum Return Date

BUDGET

My Order Placed Tracker

Order Date	Product Description	Shopping Platform	Tracking	Ship Date	Total Cost	Maximum Return Date

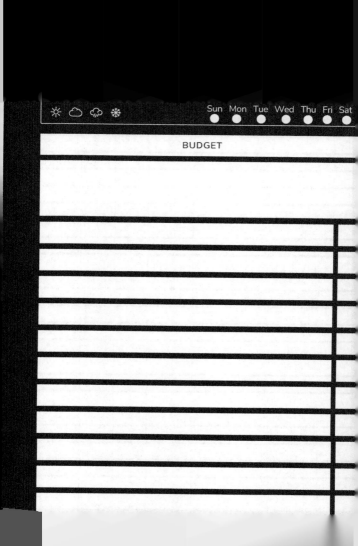

BUDGET

Sun Mon Tue Wed Thu Fri Sat

My Order Placed Tracker

Order Date	Product Description	Shopping Platform	Tracking	Ship Date	Total Cost	Maximum Return Date

Shopping List

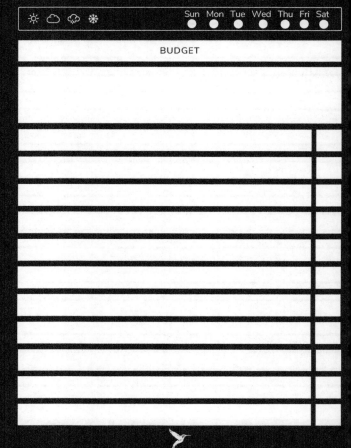

Sun Mon Tue Wed Thu Fri Sat

BUDGET

My Order Placed Tracker

Order Date	Product Description	Shopping Platform	Tracking	Ship Date	Total Cost	Maximum Return Date

My Notes

Sun Mon Tue Wed Thu Fri Sat
●   ●   ●   ●   ●   ●   ●

BUDGET

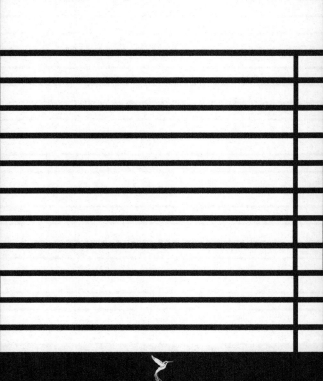

My Order Placed Tracker

Order Date	Product Description	Shopping Platform	Tracking	Ship Date	Total Cost	Maximum Return Date

Shopping List

BUDGET

My Order Placed Tracker

Order Date	Product Description	Shopping Platform	Tracking	Ship Date	Total Cost	Maximum Return Date

My Notes

BUDGET

My Order Placed Tracker

Order Date	Product Description	Shopping Platform	Tracking	Ship Date	Total Cost	Maximum Return Date

Shopping List

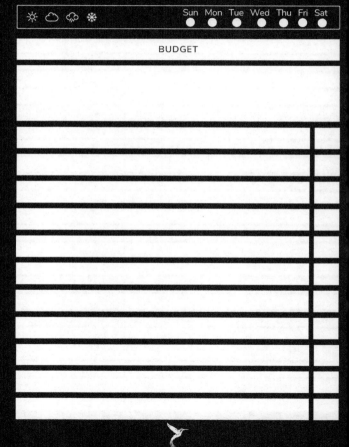

☀ ☁ ⛆ ❄	Sun Mon Tue Wed Thu Fri Sat

BUDGET

My Order Placed Tracker

Order Date	Product Description	Shopping Platform	Tracking	Ship Date	Total Cost	Maximum Return Date

My Notes

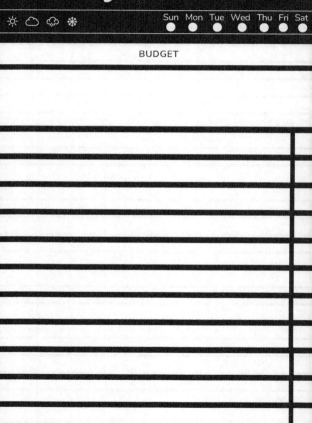

BUDGET

My Order Placed Tracker

Order Date	Product Description	Shopping Platform	Tracking	Ship Date	Total Cost	Maximum Return Date

Shopping List

☀ ☁ ☂ ❄	Sun Mon Tue Wed Thu Fri Sat

BUDGET	

My Order Placed Tracker

Order Date	Product Description	Shopping Platform	Tracking	Ship Date	Total Cost	Maximum Return Date

BUDGET

My Order Placed Tracker

Order Date	Product Description	Shopping Platform	Tracking	Ship Date	Total Cost	Maximum Return Date

Shopping List

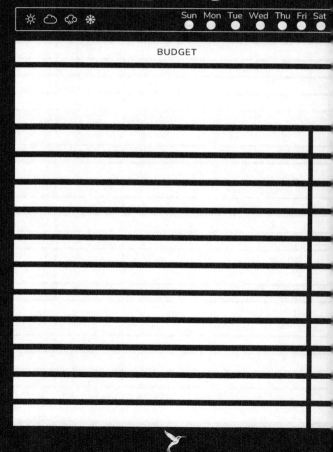

☀ ☁ ☂ ❄		Sun Mon Tue Wed Thu Fri Sat

BUDGET

My Order Placed Tracker

Order Date	Product Description	Shopping Platform	Tracking	Ship Date	Total Cost	Maximum Return Date

My Order Placed Tracker

Order Date	Product Description	Shopping Platform	Tracking	Ship Date	Total Cost	Maximum Return Date

My Notes

☼ ☁ ☂ ❄   Sun Mon Tue Wed Thu Fri Sat
                 ●   ●   ●   ●   ●   ●   ●

BUDGET

My Order Placed Tracker

Order Date	Product Description	Shopping Platform	Tracking	Ship Date	Total Cost	Maximum Return Date

Shopping List

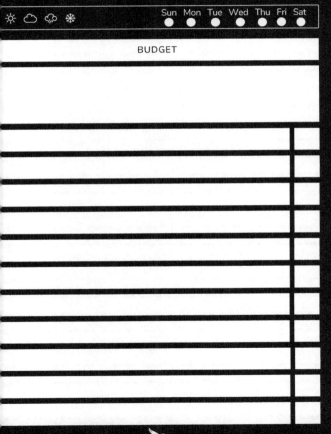

☀ ☁ ☂ ❄	Sun	Mon	Tue	Wed	Thu	Fri	Sat
	●	●	●	●	●	●	●

BUDGET

My Order Placed Tracker

Order Date	Product Description	Shopping Platform	Tracking	Ship Date	Total Cost	Maximum Return Date

My Notes

BUDGET

ONLINE SHOPPING SUMMARY TRACKER

MONTH OF

#	1	2	3	4	5	6	7	8	9	10	11	12	13	14	15	16	17	18	19	20	21	22	23	24	25	26	27	28	29	30	31
1																															
2																															
3																															
4																															
5																															
6																															
7																															
8																															
9																															
10																															
11																															
12																															
13																															
14																															
15																															
16																															
17																															
18																															
19																															
20																															
21																															
22																															
23																															
24																															
25																															
26																															
27																															
28																															
29																															
30																															

The Wisdom of an Older Man

An older man approached an attractive younger woman at a shopping mall.

"Excuse me; I can't seem to find my wife. Can you talk to me for a couple of minutes?"

The woman, feeling a bit of compassion for the old fellow, said, *"Of course, sir. Do you know where your wife might be?"*

"I have no idea, but every time I talk to a pretty woman, she seems to appear out of nowhere."

Source: https://upjoke.com/shopping-mall-joke

EXPENSE TRACKER

DATE	AMOUNT	CATEGORY	OUTGOING

NOTES

SAVINGS TRACKER

SAVING FOR	AMOUNT
START DATE	END DATE

MONTH OF		YEAR	
DATE	DESCRIPTION	SOURCE	AMOUNT

My credentials to online shopping

Marketplace	login	password	notes
Amazon			
Americanas			
Alibaba			
AliExpress			
Allegro			
Argos			
Best Buy			
Bonanza			
Canadiantire			
Coppel			
Costco			
Cratejoy			
Craigslist			
Donedeal			
eBay			
Etsy			
Flipkart			
Google Express			
Gumtree			
Hepsiburada			
Houzz			
JD			
Jet			
Kakaku			
Kijiji			

My credentials to online shopping

Marketplace	login	password	notes
Market Yandex			
Mediaexpert			
Mercadolibre			
Mercadolivre			
Mercari			
Newegg			
OLX			
Ozon			
Pinduoduo			
Rakuten			
Reverb			
Sahibinden			
Sears			
Shopee			
Shopify			
Shopping Yahoo			
Taobao			
Target			
Tmall			
Trendyol			
Walmart			
Wayfair			
Wish			
Other 1			
Other 2			

My secret credentials

web address

username/login

password

security question

notes

web address

username/login

password

security question

notes

My secret credentials

web address

username/login

password

security question

notes

---

web address

username/login

password

security question

notes

My custom

LOGBOOK

My custom

LOGBOOK

Dear Customer!

Thank you for purchasing this book. I hope you will enjoy it
I would love to hear from you any thoughts, feedback and
opinions, so I could improve my future products.

If you would like to get a free gift or have a question please
do not hesitate to contact me at: MrPinkyFox@gmail.com

Please check also my other books on Amazon:

https://tinyurl.com/PinkyFox

MR Pinky Fox

My pocket password book
WITH ALPHABETICAL TABS

Pocket password keeper

https://tinyurl.com/PinkyFox